◫ READERS

Pre-level 1

Fishy Tales
Colorful Days
Garden Friends
Party Fun
In the Park
Farm Animals
Petting Zoo
Let's Make Music
Meet the Dinosaurs
Duck Pond Dip

My Dress-up Box
On the Move
Snakes Slither and Hiss
Family Vacation
Ponies and Horses
John Deere: Busy Tractors
Lego Duplo: On the Farm
Cuentos de Peces *en español*
Dias Ilenos de color *en español*

Level 1

A Day at Greenhill Farm
Truck Trouble
Tale of a Tadpole
Surprise Puppy!
Duckling Days
A Day at Seagull Beach
Whatever the Weather
Busy Buzzy Bee
Big Machines
Wild Baby Animals
A Bed for the Winter
Born to be a Butterfly
Dinosaur's Day
Feeding Time
Diving Dolphin
Rockets and Spaceships
My Cat's Secret
First Day at Gymnastics
A Trip to the Zoo
I Can Swim!
A Trip to the Library
A Trip to the Doctor
A Trip to the Dentist
I Want to be a Ballerina
Animal Hide and Seek
Submarines and Submersibles
Animals at Home
Let's Play Soccer

Homes Around the World
LEGO: Trouble at the Bridge
LEGO: Secret at Dolphin Bay
Star Wars: What is a Wookie?
Star Wars: Ready, Set, Podrace!
Star Wars: Luke Skywalker's Amazing
    Story
Star Wars The Clone Wars: Watch Out
    for Jabba the Hutt!
Star Wars The Clone Wars: Pirates...
    and Worse
Star Wars: Tatooine Adventures
Power Rangers: Jungle Fury: We are the
    Power Rangers
Lego Duplo: Around Town
Indiana Jones: Indy's Adventures
John Deere: Good Morning, Farm!
A Day in the Life of a Builder
A Day in the Life of a Dancer
A Day in the Life of a Firefighter
A Day in the Life of a Teacher
A Day in the Life of a Musician
A Day in the Life of a Doctor
A Day in the Life of a Police Officer
A Day in the Life of a TV Reporter
Gigantes de Hierro *en español*
Crías del mundo animal *en español*

A Note to Parents

DK READERS is a compelling program for beginning readers, designed in conjunction with leading literacy experts, including Dr. Linda Gambrell, Professor of Education at Clemson University. Dr. Gambrell has served as President of the National Reading Conference and the College Reading Association, and has recently been elected to serve as President of the International Reading Association.

Beautiful illustrations and superb full-color photographs combine with engaging, easy-to-read stories to offer a fresh approach to each subject in the series. Each DK READER is guaranteed to capture a child's interest while developing his or her reading skills, general knowledge, and love of reading.

The five levels of DK READERS are aimed at different reading abilities, enabling you to choose the books that are exactly right for your child:

Pre-level 1: Learning to read
Level 1: Beginning to read
Level 2: Beginning to read alone
Level 3: Reading alone
Level 4: Proficient readers

The "normal" age at which a child begins to read can be anywhere from three to eight years old. Adult participation through the lower levels is very helpful for providing encouragement, discussing storylines, and sounding out unfamiliar words.

No matter which level you select, you can be sure that you are helping your child learn to read, then read to learn!

LONDON, NEW YORK, MUNICH,
MELBOURNE, AND DELHI

For Dorling Kindersley
Senior Editor Elizabeth Dowsett
Managing Art Editor Ron Stobbart
Managing Editor Catherine Saunders
Brand Manager Lisa Lanzarini
Publishing Manager Simon Beecroft
Category Publisher Alex Allan
Production Editor Siu Yin Chan
Production Controller Rita Sinha
Reading Consultant Dr. Linda Gambrell

For Lucasfilm
Executive Editor J. W. Rinzler
Art Director Troy Alders
Keeper of the Holocron Leland Chee
Director of Publishing Carol Roeder

Designed and edited by Tall Tree Ltd
Designer Jonathan Vipond
Editor Rob Colson

First published in the United States in 2010
by DK Publishing
375 Hudson Street, New York, New York 10014

10 11 12 13 14   10 9 8 7 6 5 4 3 2 1

DK books are available at special discounts when purchased in bulk
for sales promotions, premiums, fund-raising, or educational use.
For details, contact:
DK Publishing Special Markets
375 Hudson Street, New York, New York 10014
SpecialSales@dk.com

A catalog record for this book is available
from the Library of Congress.

ISBN: 978-0-7566-6692-7 (Paperback)
ISBN: 978-0-7566-6879-2 (Hardback)

Reproduced by Media Development and Printing Ltd., UK
Printed and bound in the United States by
Lake Book Manufacturing, Inc.

Discover more at:
www.dk.com
www.starwars.com

Contents

4   Blast off!

6   Anakin

8   R2-D2

10   C-3PO

12   Padmé

14   Obi-Wan

16   Yoda

18   Jar Jar Binks

20   Luke

22   Leia

24   Han

26   Chewbacca

28   Darth Vader

30   Heroes and villains

32   Glossary

DK READERS

LEARNING
pre-level
1
TO READ

Blast Off!

Get ready to meet some exciting people and creatures.

5... 4... 3... 2... 1...

Blast off!

Meet Anakin Skywalker.
He is a Jedi Knight.

lightsaber

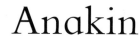
Anakin

Meet R2-D2.
He is a droid.
He can fix other droids.

R2-D2

Meet C-3PO.
He is a droid.
He can speak many
languages.

 C-3PO

Padmé

Meet Padmé Amidala.
She is a Senator.

Obi-Wan

Meet Obi-Wan Kenobi. He is a Jedi Master.

beard

Meet Yoda. He is the most powerful Jedi.

Yoda

**walking
stick**

Meet Jar Jar Binks.
He is very clumsy.

ears

Jar Jar Binks

Meet Luke Skywalker. He is a good pilot.

cape

Luke

Meet Leia Organa.
She is a Princess.

uniform

Leia

blaster

Han

Meet Han Solo.
He is a pilot.
He flies a fast ship.

Meet Chewbacca.
He is a brave co-pilot.

fur

Chewbacca

Darth Vader

Meet Darth Vader.
He is a powerful villain.

helmet

Now you have met everyone.

Who is your favorite?

Glossary

Droid

another word for a robot

Jedi

a person who can use the Force

Lightsaber

a special sword with a blade made of light

Senator

a member of the galactic government

Villain

a bad person

DK READERS

My name is

_____

I have read this book

Date

_____